LONDON IN THE SIXTIES

LONDON
IN
THE
SIXTIES

EDITED BY
GEORGE PERRY

PAVILION

Picture Editor: Suzanne Hodgart
Art Director: Grant Scott

First published in Great Britain in 2001 by
PAVILION BOOKS LIMITED
London House, Great Eastern Wharf
Parkgate Road, London SW11 4NQ
www.pavilionbooks.co.uk

Photographic copyrights and credits are detailed on pages 123–127

A CIP catalogue record for this book is available from the British Library.

ISBN 1 86205 406 1

Colour reproduction by Bright Arts, Hong Kong
Printed and bound in Spain by Graficromo

10 9 8 7 6 5 4 3 2 1

This book can be ordered direct from the publisher. Please contact
the Marketing Department. But try your bookshop first.

Opposite: World Cup euphoria, but it's all over now

n many ways it was a glorious interlude, the moment of release when the teacher leaves the room and the class realizes it is on temporary licence. London of the 1960s luxuriated in change. Restrictive traditions that once seemed impervious to reform foundered. The Lord Chamberlain ceased to decree what could be presented on the London stage. The Lady Chatterley trial disintegrated into farce. Homosexuality between consenting adults was no longer a criminal offence. Freedoms, taken for granted in other democracies, were being won without society collapsing in ruins. Not that it was entirely painless. The Profumo scandal of 1963 finished off a Tory government, thrown out after thirteen years at the 1964 general election. The dismissed Prime Minister, the affable aristocrat Alec Douglas-Home, was the last Conservative grandee to lead the party. Henceforth only grammar-school meritocrats needed to apply.

The political upheaval was not simply due to a cabinet minister having a fling with a prostitute. The new Left had skilfully used the Campaign for Nuclear Disarmament as a vehicle to promote an attractive cause. Trafalgar Square would fill with Aldermaston marchers, pilgrims who had tramped the distance between London and the atomic research centre in Berkshire where weapons of mass destruction were created. The authorities disliked the protestors and sent in baton-wielding police, but the arrests of many famous literary figures (including, notably, the imprisonment of Lord Bertrand Russell) ensured plenty of publicity critical of the government. In 1968 as the decade neared its conclusion, and other places in the world – Paris, Prague, Chicago – erupted in shockwaves of violence and disorder, Grosvenor Square was besieged by rioters at the American embassy, with more police baton squads and more celebrity arrests.

Protesting mobs in the streets are not a common British phenomenon. In London such occurrences in the twentieth century could be counted on one hand with fingers to spare. The British revolution of the 1960s was a low-key affair, tempered by the awkward realization that Harold Wilson's Labour government was, once in office, as committed to the status quo as its predecessors. The watershed of postwar British politics had in fact occurred in the previous decade: the Suez crisis of 1956, the defining moment that made the spirit of the 1960s so potent.

Another, very different, event influencing the 1960s happened just before Suez. A rich young man (who had attended Eton, and been in the Guards) dropped out of Trinity College, Cambridge because his uncle, the proprietor of a press empire, had presented him with a high-class, ailing fashion magazine almost as a plaything. It was *The Queen*, the tycoon was Sir Edward Hulton, owner of the British photo-journalism weekly *Picture Post*, by then in decline, and the young man was Jocelyn Stephens. He gathered remarkable talents, led by Mark Boxer who had been thrown out of Cambridge a year earlier for publishing a poem deemed to have been blasphemous. Boxer attracted witty writers and fresh-eyed photographers, applying stunning art direction and an unerring finger on the pulse of fashion. *Picture Post* died in 1957, and *Queen* (as it was renamed) defined itself as the new visual magazine, its circulation relatively small, but its influence pervasive. At the end of 1961 Denis Hamilton, editor of *The Sunday Times* recommended that his Canadian proprietor Roy Thomson appoint Boxer editor of the new weekly colour supplement that the newspaper intended to introduce in February 1962.

Thomson's initiative had a far-reaching effect. British newspapers had for years been restricted in size by newsprint rationing, only formally ended in the mid-1950s. Its duration was in part a cosy arrangement for both proprietors and the unions who did not want to unleash damaging circulation wars. One of the national dailies, *The News Chronicle*, had in fact been forced to close in 1961 for lack of support, but had already been supplanted by *The Guardian* which dropped the word 'Manchester' from its title in 1959 to signify its assumption of the status of a London daily. What Thomson had done was to furnish a remarkable graphic medium for reporting the age.

The Canadian Roy Thomson was reared in the tradition of multi-sectioned North American newspapers. The reaction of his newspaper rivals was scornful. His project could never work and would last only weeks. When it was seen that he had created one of the most efficient revenue-generating machines in the British press they had to copy.

Popular culture in Britain flourished as never before, with London as its epicentre. In the field of pop music Liverpool had been pre-eminent, led by The Beatles.

In the freezing winter of 1962–63 a back room in the nondescript Station Hotel in Richmond was the launch pad for a London band which outlasted not only The Beatles but almost every other rock-pop group in history. The Rolling Stones are still extant at the millennium.

New painters burst upon the scene. Hockney, a native of Bradford, graduated from the Royal College and acquired almost instant culthood. Peter Blake, Allen Jones and Bridget Riley explored new forms. Robert Fraser ran a gallery of contemporary young artists, attracting as much notoriety as if they were pop stars.

The British cinema boomed artistically early in the decade as Tony Richardson. Karel Reisz, Lindsay Anderson, John Schlesinger and others sprang to prominence. London studios were used by Americans: Stanley Kubrick who decided to stay permanently, Joseph Losey who had been kicked out of Hollywood but made his best films such as *The Servant* and *Accident in Britain*.

In theatre Pinter, Bond, and Osborne had supplanted Coward and Rattigan, now regarded as irretrievably genteel. The removal of the absurd ritual by which the Lord Chamberlain, an official with no other prescribed public duties, was empowered to censor everything that appeared on stage, and who had complained that a plank in a Frank Norman's musical *Fings Ain't What They Used to Be* was held at an obscene angle, opened up wondrous possibilities. Within a short time a nude cast was cavorting in Ken Tynan's revue *Oh Calcutta!*, a punning title that sounded in French like 'Oh, what a cute arse'.

Literary censorship collapsed when Penguin were prosecuted for publishing D. H. Lawrence's *Lady Chatterley's Lover*, a novel long unavailable in Britain on grounds of obscenity. Notoriously, the prosecuting counsel in addressing the jury asked if they would allow their wives and servants to read such a book, indicating that his world was remote from theirs. He produced no witnesses, believing his case to be complete. The defence had hundreds of witnesses of whom only a fraction needed to be called. As the trial progressed it became clear that it was not just basic words to describe the sex act that had riled the establishment, but the plot itself, in which the wife of a nobleman impotent from war wounds has a fling with his gamekeeper, thus not only cuckolding her husband but crossing the class divide.

In broadcasting it was harder to secure change in spite of heroic efforts by Hugh Greene, one of the most imaginative director generals in BBC history. Under his aegis the satirical Saturday night programme *That Was the Week That Was* provided opportunities for young comedians to lampoon entrenched attitudes. The excuse of the 1964 general election was used to drive the programme off the air, and Greene was later made to suffer an enemy, Dr Charles Hill, as his chairman.

The satire movement prospered in London in the early 1960s. Peter Cook, one of the *Beyond the Fringe* quartet, co-founded the satirical fortnightly *Private Eye* and opened The Establishment, a Soho equivalent of the continental nightclubs in which wry, witty barbs were directed against the politicians.

The evolution of so-called 'Swinging London' was largely due to fashion. Towards the middle of the decade, hemlines rose until skirts were little more than pelmets covering the front and buttocks. Mini-skirts proliferated, girls abandoning stockings and girdles for tights or pantyhose, provoking a revolution in the hosiery industry. The emphasis on legs was remarkable. Even the royals followed the trend. Princess Anne carried it off but when the Queen attempted a hemline three inches above the knee, the national shock was so great that it never recurred. London designers attracted world attention and the Kings Road, Chelsea was not only a centre for their boutiques, with names such as Skin, Granny Takes a Trip and Stop the Shop, but provided a promenade for customers. Carnaby Street, a narrow thoroughfare east of Regent Street in the West End became the tourists' centre for London fashions and ancillary souvenirs. Eventually Westminster Council pedestrianized the short street, paving it with a rubber surface bearing a garish psychedelic pattern.

It was the age of the photographer. In 1965 Francis Wyndham, a colleague of Mark Boxer at *Queen* who had followed him to *The Sunday Times*, wrote a seminal article showing how photography was fundamental to the age. Using three prominent fashion photographers as his examples, each an ambitious London lad with eyes acutely focused on every latest trend, Wyndham perceived them as part of the fabric of the times. Their work went far beyond fashion. Celebrities of the day posed readily, from movie stars to the notorious Kray twins, the East End gangsters whose reign of terror ended in long prison sentences. In David Bailey's stylish box of pin-ups they can be found alongside glamorous images of Jean Shrimpton,

Julie Christie and Twiggy. The cult of the London photographer prompted the Italian film director Michelangelo Antonioni, renowned for gnomic near-masterpieces such as *L'Avenntura*, to come to London to make *Blow Up*, its central character a photographer played by David Hemmings.

Illegal substances circulated extensively, with LSD as the wonder of the age. Even otherwise respectable middle-class dinner parties ended with joints bogarted from one diner to another. Authority was concerned. In 1967 they targeted The Rolling Stones. Mick Jagger was arrested and given six months in such feeble circumstances that it was clear he was being railroaded. *The Times*, which in the previous year had banished classified advertisements from its front page in favour of news, ran an editorial, 'Who will break a butterfly on the wheel', outlining public disquiet. The effect was Jagger's immediate release.

Hugh Greene's reign at the BBC was made difficult by the needling of Mary Whitehouse and her pressure group, the National Viewers and Listeners' Association. Similarly, John Trevelyan, secretary of the British Board of Film Censors (now Classification) attracted notoriety every time he made a decision perceived as liberal. Newspapers were plagued by so-called D-notices, preventing public discussion of any issue deemed too sensitive. Harold Evans, the liveliest broadsheet editor, talked of 'the half-free press'.

London changed its shape in the 1960s. The most radical revision of local government since Victorian times resulted in the Greater London Council, each borough formed by amalgamating older ones. Harold Wilson, back at the 1966 general election, spoke of the white heat of the technological revolution and his determination to stamp out restrictive practices that had held the nation back. The London skyline was spiked with the cranes of a construction boom. Tower blocks replaced old terraces of close-packed Victorian workmen's dwellings. A badly constructed tower block in East London collapsed in May 1968 with loss of life, damaging further high-rise development.

Even as Dr Beeching was closing swathes of the rail network at the government's behest, an ambitious plan for solving traffic congestion by girding London with a series of circular motorways was launched, but abandoned after a few short portions were found to be ineffective, having destroyed neighbourhoods yet only moving the jams from one place to another. At least the Victoria Line, the first new tube link for decades, was opened. Office blocks proliferated. The 1960s answer to Christopher Wren was Richard Seifert whose buildings, constructed from prefabricated modules, appeared throughout London. The most notorious, Centrepoint, remained tenantless for years, which was popularly perceived as a deliberate ruse to drive up its rental value.

For many, the most important 1960s occurrence was England's defeat of Germany at Wembley in the World Cup in 1966, the euphoria from which gave a boost to the re-election of Harold Wilson's Labour government that October.

**Previous pages:
Leader of the
opposition Harold
Wilson, yet to be
Prime Minister,
poses with
The Beatles**

**Left: Vidal Sassoon,
top hairdresser,
crimps Mary Quant**

**Right: Bazaar duo,
Mary Quant and
Alexander Plunkett
Greene**

David Bailey gets his subject in the mood and shares a sofa with model Penelope Tree

Left: Ballroom couples
await the next dance

Right: Evening date – a
flat-sharing girl prepares

Overleaf: Model Jean
Shrimpton 'the Shrimp'
and Terence Stamp,
film star

Above: Model and fashion editor Grace Coddington with Mark Boxer, magazine editor

Right: Carnaby Street Pop Café and Triumph coupé

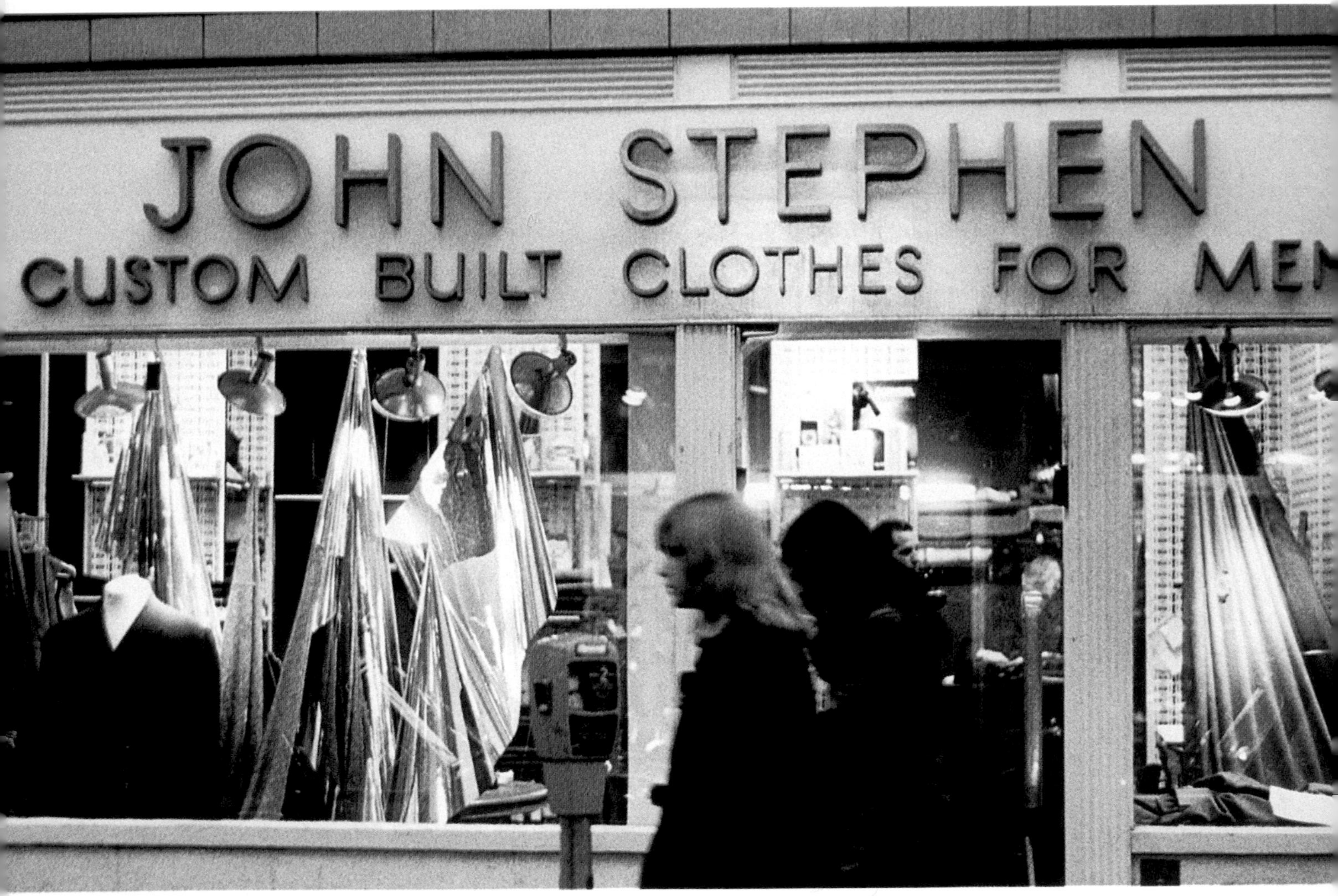
JOHN STEPHEN
CUSTOM BUILT CLOTHES FOR ME

Left: Carnaby Street chic behind a boring facade

Right: Unappreciated art – Robert Fraser goes to court

Overleaf (left): Christine Keeler dines out with Ronnie Kray and chums. And right, Mandy Rice-Davies with Keeler in tow, faces the cameras during the Stephen Ward trial

**Stars Sue Lyon and Peter Sellers
at the premiere of
Stanley Kubrick's *Lolita***

Left: Royal Court Theatre,
the theatrical Mecca

Right: Ken Tynan, literati darling

Below: Bond actor Sean Connery pushes vodka for ad campaign

Right: New star Michael Caine at home with his mum at the Elephant and Castle

**Left: Ian Fleming,
James Bond creator**

**Right: Len Deighton,
the creator of spy
Harry Palmer**

THE IPCRESS FILE
THE IPCRESS
SS FILE
EVENING
STANDARD
FLEet St
3000

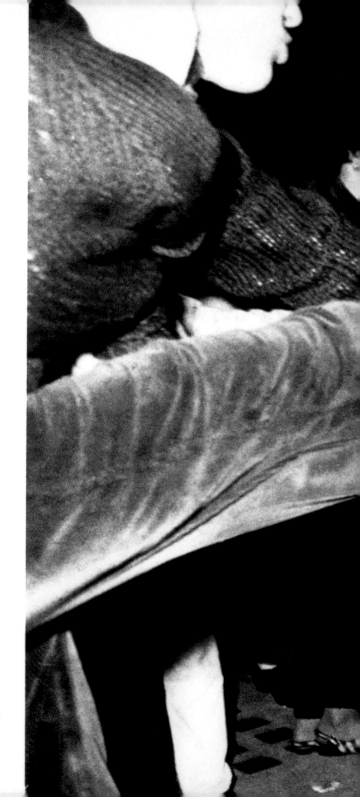

Right: The boot goes in at the Grosvenor Square riots

Overleaf: End of trial of Oz, 1960s prime underground newspaper

Left: The early editorial
team of satirical
fortnightly *Private Eye*

Right: *Beyond the Fringe*
team launches
satire movement

Above: Tony Hancock, comedian, endures a railway buffet

Right: Housewives in as yet ungentrified North Kensington

Left: Aldermaston protestors, Trafalgar Square

Right: Pop icon Adam Faith and his Rolls-Royce

42

43

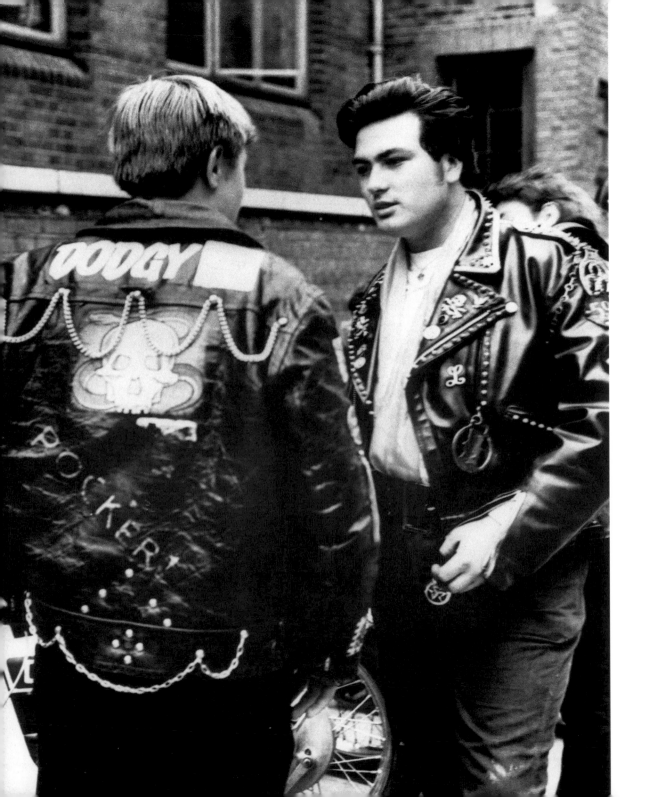

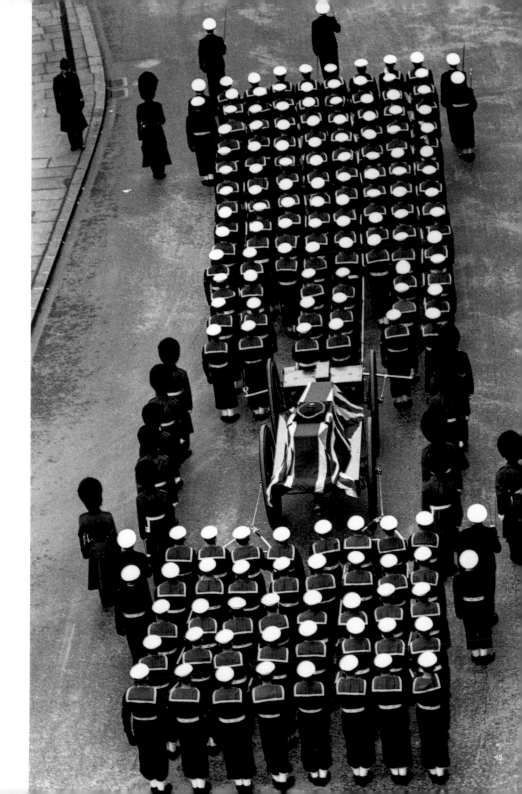

Left: New England resurgent with motor bike rockers

Right: Old England requiescat as Churchill goes to rest

45

Angry youth at Rolling Stones concert in Hyde Park

Dramatists (from left to right), N F Simpson, Harold Pinter and John Mortimer

Dolly bird on the Kings Road (left) and mods on scooters in Brixton (middle), and wearing winkle-pickers (right)

**Mods on scooters rally
for ride to coast**

On Kings Road, chic couple
(left) and trendy café (right)

Piccadilly Circus protest

Left: Grabbed, a Grosvenor Square protester

Right: Andrew Loog Oldham, pop promoter, record company owner and manager of The Rolling Stones

Left: Busted – Brian Jones of
The Rolling Stones leaves court

Right: Trying it on – a customer
at the super-boutique Biba

Overleaf: *Darling* girl,
actress Julie Christie

Left: Singer, Sandie Shaw

Right: Fashion designer,
Jean Muir

**Pop art leaders Peter Blake (above)
and David Hockney (right)**

**Overleaf: The Beatles arrive at Buckingham
Palace to collect their MBEs**

Arnold Wesker, playwright (left) and above, Peter O'Toole, actor

Left: *Billy Liar* playwrights
Keith Waterhouse and
Willis Hall

Right: Germaine Greer,
ultra-feminist

Left: Commuters on London Bridge

Right: Twiggy models a halterneck

Above: Artist Joe Tilson

Left: Minimalist Mini decoration

Bridget Riley, op artist

Left: Centrepoint, the 1960s
capitalist icon

Right: Allen Jones, artist accused
of fetishising women

Left: Keith Moon drummer with The Who

Above: Pete Townshend singer, songwriter and lead guitarist also of The Who

**Far left: Who guitarist
John Entwistle at home
with his mum**

**Left: Who vocalist Roger
Daltrey in digs with discs**

Above: The Kinks (*Waterloo
Sunset***) in action**

(Left to right): Newspaper seller; a demo at the LSE; vending underground newspaper *IT* on the street

Right: Stones in the park – Mick Jagger and the group

Below: Middle Earth Club entrance after drug bust by 150 police

Left: Lionel Bart, composer of
Oliver!, and singing protégé
Mark Wynter

Right: Apple, The Beatles shop,
Baker Street

Overleaf: Killer smog hits London

97

The boutique Granny takes a Trip on the Kings Road (left); record store in Soho (above)

**Men stare at man
for a change,
Carnaby Street**

Left: City gents chat
in passing

Right: Covent
Garden in its final
days as a produce
market

Overleaf: Car
workers claim right
to work

TORY
KEEPING PROFITS UNLOADS WORKERS
Share The Work
NO RETURN TO MASS UNEMPLOYMENT
ROOTES GROUP 12,000 DEMAND TO SHARE WORK
THERE ARE MORE MARKETS THAN IN U·S·A REMOVE TRADING RESTRICTIONS
ROOTES GROUP NO SACKINGS We Demand RIGHT TO WORK
Share The Work

Above: Conservative Prime Minister Alec Douglas-Home gives up the premiership

Left: Press executive Hugh Cudlipp launches *The Sun*

Above: Coffee bar on Old Compton Street   **Right: Theatrical innovator Joan Littlewood and actress Barbara Windsor**

Right: Girls at the fairground on Hampstead Heath

Below: Club owner and jazz man Ronnie Scott with tenor sax

Left: Rita Tushingham on stage in *The Knack*

Right: Nell Dunn, author of *Up the Junction*

**Mick Jagger and
Marianne Faithfull**

Legalize cannabis rally in Hyde Park

Anti-Vietnam war demo

PHOTO
CAPTIONS

Front cover: Twiggy, at 16 and already the fashion archetype of 1960s London, poses on a doorstep.
Popperfoto

Page 5: Was this the greatest moment in English football? In the World Cup Final at Wembley on 30 July 1966, teammates Geoff Hurst and Ray Wilson hoist their captain Bobby Moore aloft after their 4–2 triumph in the final against West Germany. In his hand is the precious Jules Rimet Trophy which was permanently awarded to the triple-winner Brazil at the succeeding contest in 1970.
Topham

Pages 10–11: Harold Wilson, Leader of the Opposition, poses with The Beatles at the 1963 Variety Club of Great Britain Awards.
Hulton Getty

Page 12: Vidal Sassoon, arbiter of hair style in the 1960s, applies his skills to the austere bob of another fashion icon, Mary Quant.
Hulton Getty

Page 13: Mary Quant and Alexander Plunkett Greene, partners in marriage and business, were influential figures on the London fashion scene, notably with the popularizing of the miniskirt. They were photographed for *Vogue* by Terence Donovan in 1962.
Terence Donovan © The Condé Nast Publications Ltd/Camera Press

Page 14: David Bailey, doyen of trendy photographers of the time, at work.
Terry O'Neill/Camera Press

Page 15: David Bailey, is photographed with his then girlfriend Penelope Tree who is wearing a heavy silver neck chain and a racoon belt. Period touches include the dial telephone, the psychedelic ornamental boot and the unabashed way in which both subjects are smoking cigarettes.
Terry O'Neill/Camera Press

Page 16: Not all young couples subscribed to the new mode of tight-packed, frenetic, unconnected, jerky bouncing to rock beats under strobe lighting. Here the traditional sartorial niceties of the ballroom are properly observed.
David Hurn/Magnum

Page 17: One of four girls sharing a flat prepares for an evening date in a bathtub festooned with stockings.
Eve Arnold/Magnum

Page 18: David Bailey's most famous photograph of the London model of the decade, Jean Shrimpton, whose super-cool, classic features and unpretentious yet shrewd fashion sense served as a role model for many less endowed women.
Hulton Getty

Page 19: Terence Stamp became a star in *Billy Budd*, and soon became an iconic British actor, seen here in *Vogue* in 1967.
The Donovan Archive/Camera Press

Page 20: Mark Boxer, then art director of *Queen* magazine and soon to become editor of Fleet Street's first regular

gravure magazine, *The Sunday Times* colour section, which was launched in 1962. He is talking to the fashion model, Grace Coddington.
Hulton Getty

Page 21: The Pop Café on Carnaby Street with a snazzy Triumph roadster at the parking meter.
Hulton Getty

Page 22: John Stephen's Carnaby Street shop front was surprisingly mundane and would not have looked out of place in a provincial high street. A deceptive impression. It was the capital's trendiest men's clothing emporium and scores of prominent figures, be they icons of entertainment and fashion or leaders of the underworld, crossed its threshold.
Rex Features

Page 23: The adage that everyone is a critic had heavy resonances for gallery owner Robert Fraser. In his case, the art critics were members of the Metropolitan Police who deemed the displayed work of the Ohio-born, innovative painter and sculptor Jim Dine, obscene. Here Fraser attends the court hearing where he was fined £20 with 50 guineas costs. In the 1960s the archaic denomination of the guinea was still applied to paintings and racehorses.
Hulton Getty

Page 24: East End gangster Ronnie Kray (middle right) and some of the boys share a table with Christine Keeler, who became a national icon for her

involvement in the 1963 Profumo scandal.
Hulton Getty

Page 25: Mandy Rice-Davies, the super-cool blonde involved in the Stephen Ward/Profumo scandal faces the cameras after her appearance at Ward's trial. Less poised behind her is Christine Keeler who was later jailed for her part in the affair which rocked Britain in 1963.
Hulton Getty

Pages 26–7: Peter Sellers with Sue Lyon at the London premiere of Stanley Kubrick's *Lolita* at the Columbia Theatre, 7 September 1962. Lyon played the title role and the versatile Sellers played Quilty in the film. Lyon, then 16, had been unable to see it earlier because in America it was banned to the under-18s.
Hulton Getty

Page 28: The Royal Court Theatre, Sloane Square, a pace-setting London theatre venue in the 1960s.
© Fred W. McDarrah

Page 29: Kenneth Tynan, critic and essayist was renowned as the first person who deliberately uttered the 'f-word' on BBC Television, in its proper sense. He was approaching the apogee of his career with the groundwork laid for the creation of the National Theatre.
Snowdon/Camera Press

Page 30: Sean Connery, selected from fierce competition to play James Bond in *Dr No*, is photographed by Terence

Donovan for a London promotion on behalf of Smirnoff Vodka.

The Donovan Archive/Camera Press

Pages 30–1: Michael Caine, about to become a star in *The Ipcress File*, pictured at home with his mother and brother at the Elephant and Castle.

Hulton Getty

Page 32: Bon viveur, well-connected gambler and international journalist, Ian Fleming created the British secret agent 007, James Bond, and for a decade published a new thriller each year. In 1962 Bond took to the screen, played by Sean Connery, in the first of the longest-lived film series ever. In the same year Fleming suddenly died.

© Loomis Dean/Timepix/Katz

Page 33: Harry Palmer was the plebeian counterpart of the patrician James Bond, an army intelligence NCO who was usually at odds with his superiors. He was the creation of the thriller writer and expert cook Len Deighton and three Palmer books were filmed.

Hulton Getty

Pages 34–5: In 1968 anti-Vietnam demonstrations echoed worldwide protest against the war. The US Embassy in Grosvenor Square was besieged, and here this policeman, unprotected by riot gear, sustains a savage headkick.

Hulton Getty

Pages 36–7: The two leading underground publications in 1960s London were the

International Times (*IT*) and *Oz*, founded by an Australian Richard Neville in February 1967. The authorities smiled on neither, disliking the aura of drug-taking and anarchy that surrounded them. Infamously, *Oz* was prosecuted for its notorious schoolkids issue, which was certainly not aimed at children. This crowd greeted the guilty verdict at the Old Bailey.

Camera Press

Page 38: Launched in October 1961, the satirical fortnightly *Private Eye*, founded by a number of old boys of Shrewsbury School and modelled on continental prototypes, began to needle the establishment from its fourth isssue. W H Smith, Britain's largest newsagent chain and distributor, banned it from its premises. This picture shows some of the editorial team in April 1965. *Back row*: Richard Ingrams, Tony Rushton, Paul Foot, Barry Fantoni and Gill Brooke; *Middle row*: Gabby Hughes, Peter Usborne; *Seated*: John Wells, unidentified, Jan Elson and Michael Whale.

© Lewis Morley/The Akehurst Bureau

Page 39: Jonathan Miller, Peter Cook, Dudley Moore and Alan Bennett, the quartet of *Beyond the Fringe*, which spearheaded the satire boom of the early 1960s.

Cecil Beaton/Camera Press

Page 40: The comedian Tony Hancock is photographed in the stressful setting of a railway refreshment room as part of a series of advertisements for British Railways. Hancock, celebrated for the lugubrious

persona he projected in character on radio and televison, committed suicide in 1968, five years after Terence Donovan took this picture.

The Donovan Collection/Camera Press

Pages 40–1: Gentrification had yet to reach to the dense streets of North Kensington where these working-class wives were photographed in 1961. The scarcity of parked cars and the prevalence of litter indicate the quality of the neighbourhood.

Roger Mayne/Mary Evans Picture Library

Page 42: Well-dressed protestors gather against the bomb at a CND rally on the plinth of Nelson's Column in Trafalgar Square in 1964.

Philip Jones Griffiths/Magnum

Page 43: Adam Faith, successful pop star and entrepreneur, is seen alongside his symbol of achievement, a Rolls-Royce.

© Lewis Morley/The Akehurst Bureau

Page 44: Rockers, the motorcycle enemies of the Mods, assemble in Stratford, East London in preparation for a ride.

Corbis–Bettmann/UPI

Page 45: The greatest Briton of the twentieth century expired aged 90 in 1965. Young guardsmen carried Winston Churchill's coffin onto a riverboat for a stately progress along the Thames. The dockside cranes that still lined the Pool of London dipped in salute as the waterborne cortege passed by.

George Rodger/Magnum

Pages 46–7: A scowling Hells Angel is among the huge audience at The Rolling Stones 1969 concert in Hyde Park.

Hulton Getty

Page 48: The team of *That Was the Week That Was* including Lance Percival (left) David Frost (kneeling), Roy Kinnear (centre) and Millicent Martin (right) caused a sensation when the show was introduced by the BBC in 1962. Sadly, only two television seasons were permitted, the excuse of the 1964 General Election enabling the powers-that-be to kill it.

Topham

Page 49: Joe Orton, a brilliant and outrageous comedy playwright convicted for homosexual cruising and defacing library books, mimics the famous Christine Keeler pose for the same photographer, Lewis Morley.

© Lewis Morley/The Akehurst Bureau

Pages 50–1: A trio of successful playwrights (from the left), N F Simpson, Harold Pinter and John Mortimer in 1966.

Hulton Getty

Page 52 (left): The look of 1967. A blonde in a minidress and boots is seen on Kings Road, her hair and make-up appropriate to the fashion of the time. As hemlines rose stockings were abandoned and were replaced by tights.

Hulton Getty

Pages 52–3 (middle and right): Rockers rode motor bikes, but their rivals, the Mods, rode scooters. Mods were usually underpaid junior office workers and scooters were not expensive, leaving enough spare cash to invest in Mod gear. They wore caps, sharp jackets and winkle-picker footwear. Generally, Mods were a South London phenomenon and these are in Brixton.

Roger Mayne/Mary Evans Picture Library

Pages 54–5: Mods on motor scooters assemble for a weekend ride to the coast. Crash helmets were not yet a legal requirement.

Topham

Page 56: Frith Street in Soho at night, with the world-famous Ronnie Scott's jazz club on the right.

Hulton Getty

Page 57: Carnaby Street's Christmas decorations in 1967 rivalled the more staid approach of Regent Street nearby.

Hulton Getty

Pages 58-9: Characteristic hairstyles of the time adorn this group of young women engaged in social chit-chat in Islington in 1964.

Roger Mayne/Mary Evans Picture Library

Page 60: Kings Road in Chelsea was the mainspring of the 'London Look' which originated around the time Mary Quant opened her Bazaar store in 1955. By the 1960s the street had become a world focus for stylish dress and chic boutiques. Here, a fashionable couple take a stroll, carefully

aware of the impression they are making.

Rex Features

Page 61: Kings Road. Chelsea, epicentre of the 'Swinging London' scene had many restaurants and cafés where the new young and affluent foregathered. The 235 placed an emphasis on its Frenchness, the ambiance being for the pleasure of its proprietor, with eating as a secondary consideration, although the window does bear the legend 'Le patron mange ici'.

Rex Features

Pages 62–3: Marchers clog Piccadilly Circus, the hub of the West End, as they exercise their democratic right of protest.

Rex Features

Page 64: A demonstration in 1968 at the US Embassy in Grosvenor Square against the war in Vietnam. Although the police were out in strength they were not equipped with riot gear, an indication that violent unrest on British streets was then comparatively rare.

Eve Arnold/Magnum

Page 65: The Rolling Stones were first encountered by Andrew Loog Oldham whilst playing in a backroom at The Station Hotel, Richmond in 1962. They were fashioned by him into London's answer to the Merseyside groups led by The Beatles. In 1965 he parted company with the band, by then established internationally at the apex of the rock-pop world.

Page 66: Stylishly suited, Brian Jones of The Rolling Stones,

leaves West London Magistrates Court in 1967 after a charge of drug possession.

Hulton Getty

Page 67: Barbara Hulanicki's store Biba was another significant element in the ready-to-wear fashion scene in 1960s London. It is especially notable for its Egyptian décor visible in this glimpse of a changing room.

Martine Franck/Magnum

Page 68: Julie Christie – the darling of British cinema in the 1960s – as captured by the celebrity photographer Terence Donovan in 1962.

The Donovan Collection/Camera Press

Page 69: Julie Christie left the Central School of Speech and Drama in London and had a couple of small comedy parts before bursting into the public consciousness with her appearance in John Schlesinger's *Billy Liar* (1962). She went on to win an Academy Award for the leading role in his film *Darling* (1965) and became an international star.

David Hurn/Magnum

Page 70: Sandie Shaw, a pop singer known for kicking her shoes off when performing, adopts her celebrated stockinged-feet pose as she models clothes in the window of her boutique.

Hulton Getty

Page 71: Jean Muir at work, one of the leading designers in the 1960s.

Topham

Page 72: Peter Blake, pop artist, is captured reviving the enamel sign techniques of Edwardian advertising.

Snowdon/Camera Press

Page 73: David Hockney, the painter who sprang to prominence in the 1960s after graduating from the Royal College of Art, is on the set of *Ubu Roi* at the Royal Court Theatre, having designed the sets for the production.

Hulton-Deutsch Collection/Corbis

Pages 74–5: Policeman struggle to contain the excitement of hordes of female fans as The Beatles call at Buckingham Palace to receive their MBEs from the Queen.

Hulton Getty

Page 76: Arnold Wesker, playwright of *The Kitchen* and *Chips with Everything*.

Snowdon/Camera Press

Page 77: Peter O'Toole takes a short rest on the opening night of *Hamlet*. His performance in David Lean's *Lawrence of Arabia* elevated him to overnight international stardom.

Eve Arnold/Magnum

Page 78: Playwrights Keith Waterhouse and Willis Hall who brought their earthy, but fashionable northern voices to the London theatre, co-wrote the successful comedy *Billy Liar*, an engaging tribute to a young fantasist that was later filmed by John Schlesinger.

© Lewis Morley/The Akehurst Bureau

Page 79: Germaine Greer, the articulate Australian feminist, gained a PhD at Cambridge and became the 1960s most outstanding spokesperson for women, culminating in the 1970 publication of her masterwork *The Female Eunuch*.

Topham

Page 80: Commuters crowd the footway of London Bridge, outpacing stalled traffic as they make their way to their City offices in the morning rush hour. Inconveniently, the large railway station of London Bridge was sited on the south side of the river in the 1830s, and the walk has been a tradition for London commuters ever since. This London Bridge is now at Lake Havasu, California, having been replaced in 1973.

Roger Mayne/Mary Evans Picture Library

Page 81: The waif-like fashion model Twiggy poses atop a sports car in a plastic see-through minidress, held up by a halterneck.

Hulton Getty

Pages 82–3: The home painting of trendy designs on cars was a popular diversionary pastime in the 1960s, and the Alex Issigonis-designed Mini, introduced in 1959, was considered the most suitable vehicle for the purpose. This restrained example of artwork on a car was spotted in Carnaby Street.

Rex Features

Page 83: Joe Tilson, who sprang to prominence in the pop-art movement, had his first one-man show at the Marlborough Gallery in 1962. In 1964 his spangly advertisement in Piccadilly Circus

commissioned by Guinness drew attention away from surrounding neon signs, without expending any electricity.

Snowdon/Camera Press

Pages 84–5: Bridget Riley, lately employed by a Berkeley Square advertising agency designing cornflakes packets, ascended to the world art stage with her intricate optical designs involving straight lines, curves, spirals, meshes. Riley's brilliance was dubbed 'op art', the scale of which could induce dizziness when viewed too long on display.

Topham

Page 86: The phallic Centrepoint, an office tower designed by Richard Seifert, sprang up at the southern end of Tottenham Court Road, then remained empty for many years, becoming a symbol to some of the decline of capitalism.

Topham

Page 87: Artist, Allen Jones was renowned for presenting sculptured women in latex bras and g-strings as items of domestic furniture.

Snowdon/Camera Press

Pages 88–9: The Who's drummer Keith Moon captured in action at a 1966 gig.

Colin Jones

Page 89: Pete Townshend of The Who, tries on a new coat at Just Men on the Kings Road.

Colin Jones

Page 90: John Entwistle of The Who strums a guitar as his mother knits.

Colin Jones

Page 91 (left): Lead singer of The Who, Roger Daltrey, listening to 45 rpm singles on his record player.

Colin Jones

Page 91 (right): The Kinks captured in action. This London pop group was led by Ray Davies and their hits included *Waterloo Sunset* and *Dedicated Follower of Fashion*.

Topham

Page 92 (left): Outside a tube station a news vendor uses an ancient perambulator to dispense his wares.

© Fred W. McDarrah

Page 92 (right): As universities around the world succumbed to a fever of sit-ins and occupations, the London School of Economics was beset in October 1968. 'The only true goal of a revolution' reads the placard on a student's back 'is the pursuit of unlicensed pleasure'. Not exactly a Marxist sentiment.

Topham

Page 93: One of a pair of street sellers offers a copy of the underground newspaper *International Times* to a young woman on Oxford Street. The coal scuttle is a mystery – unsolicited gifts, perhaps?

Topham

Page 94: The calm around the entrance to the Middle Earth Club is deceptive – earlier 150 police raided the club. Eight were charged with possession of drugs, having offensive weapons and causing police obstruction.

Corbis/Bettmann/UPI

Page 95: The Rolling Stones, prior to embarking for New York and an appearance on the *Ed Sullivan Show*, take a stroll in Green Park for the benefit of the cameras in January 1967. They are (left to right) Charlie Watts, Bill Wyman, Mick Jagger, Keith Richard and Brian Jones,

Topham

Page 96: The composer and songwriter Lionel Bart posed in Hyde Park with the 17-year-old singing discovery Mark Wynter. The intention was to publicize Bart's Autumn 1960 single *Kicking Up the Leaves*.

Tom Blau/Camera Press

Page 97: The Beatles joined the boutique revolution by establishing their Apple shop on Baker Street. Its striking psychedelic decoration disturbed local residents and lasted for only a short time.

Topham

Pages 98–9: Killer smogs were once a London scourge, accelerating the deaths of many whose respiratory functions were too weak to cope. One of the last was in December 1962 when more than 40 people died from the fumes. The disappearance of coal-burning fires eventually ended the hazard.

Topham

Page 100: A colourful storefront on Kings Road, the main street of Chelsea which became an axis for 'Swinging London'.

Rex Features

Page 101: A record shop in Soho attracts nocturnal window browsers.
Hulton Getty

Pages 102–3: Men often stare at girls on the street, but more rarely at boys. This youth, dressed to the nines in 'Carnaby Street style', attracts considerable attention from a more conventionally attired masculine group, observed by the camera on the street in question.
Topham

Page 104: Two bowler-hatted businessmen have a conversation outside a Regent Street shop. The setting is the West End, but their attire is more characteristic of the City.
© Fred W. McDarrah

Page 105: Covent Garden in 1960, a busy fruit and vegetable market in the heart of the West End, and at its busiest in the hours preceding the commuter rush.
Topham

Pages 106–7: Car workers demonstrate in London following a wave of redundancies in 1960. Rootes, manufacturers of Hillman, Singer and Sunbeam-Talbot, is one of the long-vanished giants of the British motor industry.
Topham

Page 108: The newspaper executive Hugh Cudlipp presided over the demise of the *Daily Herald* and its transformation into *The Sun* in 1964. Cudlipp's broadsheet newspaper was not as successful as had been hoped and was sold to the Australian media tycoon Rupert Murdoch, who transformed it into a snappy tabloid on the lines of the *Daily Mirror*.
Topham

Page 109: Conservative leader, Sir Alec Douglas-Home, looks positvely relieved to be out of the hot seat having just handed in his resignation as Prime Minister at Buckingham Palace after the 1964 election, won by Harold Wilson's Labour Party.
Topham

Page 110: The 2is coffee bar on Old Compton Street in Soho had achieved modest fame in the 1960s as a hangout for aspirant pop stars, having achieved fame in the previous decade as the place where Tommy Steele was discovered.
Topham

Page 111: Joan Littlewood, director of Theatre Workshop, talks to the actress Barbara Windsor shortly before departure on an American tour of her hugely successful *Oh! What a Lovely War*.
Topham

Page 112: Ronnie Scott plays tenor sax in a set at his own jazz club, Dean Street, Soho, in between regaling the audience with his characteristic repartee.
Topham

Page 113: Dolly birds at the Hampstead Heath Bank Holiday fair in 1961. The vogue for knitted cardigans over buttoned-up, coloured tennis shirts, teased hair and sunglasses was the customary look for working and lower middle-class girls that summer.
Roger Mayne/Mary Evans Picture Library

Page 114: Rita Tushingham was the only member of the theatre cast of Ann Jellicoe's *The Knack*, staged at the Royal Court in 1962, to appear in the later film version, directed by Richard Lester. Others in the original production (left to right) are Philip Locke, Julian Glover and James Bolam.
Camera Press

Page 115: Nell Dunn, daughter of a millionaire baronet, turned her back on riches to live in a working-class section of Battersea, taking a job in a local sweets factory. The experience led to her vivid novels on the lives of the poor, *Up the Junction* and *Poor Cow*, both of which became successful films. The author then moved to the more genteel area of Putney.
Camera Press

Pages 116–17: Two of the icons of the age, Mick Jagger of The Rolling Stones whose high-energy vocal performances assisted the group's lift-off into the stratosphere of rock, and Marianne Faithfull, doleful singer of such hits as *Come and Stay with Me*.
John Kelly/Camera Press

Pages 118–19: Thousands gathered in Hyde Park in 1968 in a cheerful campaign to legalize cannabis. Decades later their wishes are still unfulfilled.
Topham

Page 120–1: Anti-Vietnam war protestors gather in Piccadilly Circus, echoing similar demonstrations in the United States. Harold Wilson, the British Prime Minister for much of the 1960s, kept his nation out of the war.
Philip Jones-Griffith/Magnum

Back cover: Frith Street in Soho at night.
Hulton Getty